Empowering Wealth!

52 WEEKS
OF
DEVOTIONS

FOR

YOUR
FINANCIAL
SUCCESS!

Empowering Wealth!

52 WEEKS OF DEVOTIONS

FOR

YOUR FINANCIAL SUCCESS!

DR. G.R. QUARLES, MBA, DBA
AHQ PUBLISHING, LLC

ISBN: 9798859287208
Printed in the United States of America

Dr. G.R. Quarles, MBA, DBA
President of AHQ Publishing LLC
Author, Speaker, Consultant, Professor
P.O. Box 1221
Tappahannock, VA 22560
Email: ahqpublishingllc@gmail.com
Website: AHQPUBLISHINGLLC.COM

Epigraph

"*M*ay these devotions illuminate your path to financial empowerment. As you journey through the weeks, may you unlock the keys to abundance, discover the treasures within your reach, and forge a future rich with possibilities. Let the wisdom within these pages guide you towards the prosperous life you deserve."

52 WEEKS
OF
DEVOTIONS

Week 1

Gratitude for Abundance

This week, take a moment to acknowledge the wealth that surrounds you. True wealth goes beyond material possessions; it encompasses health, relationships, and opportunities. Practice gratitude for the abundance in your life, and as you cultivate an attitude of appreciation, you'll attract more blessings to be grateful for.

My Notes for Gratitude for Abundance

_____

_____

_____

_____

_____

_____

My Weekly Prayer

I Pray for Gratitude for Abundance!

Week 2

Cultivating a Growth Mindset

This week, embrace a growth mindset when it comes to wealth. See challenges as opportunities for learning and growth. By viewing setbacks as steppingstones to success, you'll develop resilience and the ability to adapt to changing circumstances, ultimately enhancing your financial journey.

My Notes for Cultivating a Growth Mindset

_____

_____

_____

_____

_____

My Weekly Prayer

I Pray for Cultivating a Growth Mindset!

Week 3

Setting Clear Financial Goals

*T*his week define your financial aspirations clearly. Whether it's saving for a dream vacation, buying a home, or starting a business, specific goals provide direction and purpose. Break these goals into actionable steps and watch how your intentions guide your efforts toward achieving lasting wealth.

My Notes for Setting Clear Financial Goals

_____

_____

_____

_____

_____

_____

My Weekly Prayer

I Pray for Setting Clear Financial Goals!

Week 4

Embracing Abundance Mentality

This week, shift from a scarcity mindset to an abundance mentality. Recognize that there is more than enough wealth and success to go around. Celebrate the accomplishments of others, knowing that their success doesn't diminish your potential. Embracing abundance opens the door to collaboration and limitless possibilities.

My Notes for Embracing Abundance Mentality

_____

_____

_____

_____

_____

_____

My Weekly Prayer

I Pray for Embracing Abundance Mentality!

Week 5

Investing in Self Development

This week, investing in your personal growth is a powerful way to enhance your wealth. Learn new skills, expand your knowledge, and continuously improve. Your abilities are valuable assets that can lead to increased opportunities, higher income, and a more prosperous life.

My Notes for Investing in Self Development

_____

_____

_____

_____

_____

My Weekly Prayer

I Pray for Investing in Self Development!

Week 6

Practicing Financial Discipline

This week, I will practice disciplined financial habits. Budget wisely, live within your means, and prioritize saving. Avoid impulsive purchases and seek value in experiences rather than possessions. Over time, small daily choices will contribute to a secure and empowered financial future.

My Notes for Practicing Financial Discipline

_____

_____

_____

_____

_____

_____

My Weekly Prayer

I Pray for Practicing Financial Discipline!

Week 7

Exploring Multiple Streams of Income

This week, diversify your sources of income to create a stable foundation for wealth. Consider starting a side business, investing in stocks, or exploring freelancing opportunities. Multiple streams of income provide security and open the door to greater financial potential.

My Notes for Exploring Multiple Streams of Income

_____

_____

_____

_____

_____

_____

My Weekly Prayer

I Pray for Exploring Multiple Streams of Income!

Week 8

Overcoming Financial Fears

This week, identify and confront your financial fears. Whether it's fear of failure or fear of taking risks, addressing these emotions can liberate you from their constraints and empower you to make confident financial decisions.

My Notes for Overcoming Financial Fears

_____

_____

_____

_____

_____

_____

_____

My Weekly Prayer

I Pray for Overcoming Financial Fears!

Week 9

Practicing Generosity

This week, practice giving without expecting anything in return. Generosity aligns you with the flow of abundance and creates positive energy around wealth. Whether through charitable donations, acts of kindness, or sharing your knowledge, your generosity will come back to you in unexpected ways.

My Notes for Practicing Generosity

_____

_____

_____

_____

_____

_____

My Weekly Prayer

I Pray for Practicing Generosity!

Week 10

Harnessing the Law of Attraction

This week, harness the law of attraction to manifest your financial desires. Visualize your goals with clarity and focus, believing that you are worthy of the wealth you seek. By aligning your thoughts and feelings with your intentions, you can attract opportunities and resources that lead to financial empowerment.

My Notes for Harnessing the Law of Attraction

_____

_____

_____

_____

_____

My Weekly Prayer

I Pray for Harnessing the Law of Attraction!

Week 11

Building Resilience in Adversity

Financial challenges are inevitable. Build resilience by staying adaptable and focused on solutions. Remember that setbacks are temporary, and your ability to overcome them strengthens your path toward lasting wealth.

My Notes for Building Resilience in Adversity

_____

_____

_____

_____

_____

_____

My Weekly Prayer

I Pray for Building Resilience in Adversity!

Week 12

Networking for Success

Cultivate meaningful relationships within your industry and community. Networking provides opportunities for collaboration, mentorship, and knowledge-sharing. As you connect with others, you'll discover new avenues for growth and empowerment.

My Notes for Networking for Success

_____

_____

_____

_____

_____

_____

My Weekly Prayer

I Pray for Networking for Success!

Week 13

Navigating Risk Wisely

Risk is a part of wealth-building, but it's essential to approach it wisely. Educate yourself about potential risks and rewards and make informed decisions. Balancing calculated risks with prudent choices will lead you toward financial empowerment.

My Notes for Navigating Risk Wisely

_____

_____

_____

_____

_____

_____

_____

My Weekly Prayer

I Pray for Navigating Risk Wisely!

Week 14

Transforming Mindset around Money

Examine your beliefs about money and wealth. Are they limiting or empowering? Transform any negative beliefs into positive affirmations that align with your financial aspirations. A transformed mindset can accelerate your journey toward prosperity.

My Notes for Transforming Mindset around Money

_____

_____

_____

_____

_____

_____

My Weekly Prayer

I Pray for Transforming Mindset around Money!

Week 15

Cultivating Patience and Persistence

*W*ealth-building takes time and consistent effort. Cultivate patience and persistence as you work toward your goals. Remember that small, consistent actions accumulate to create significant results over time.

My Notes for Cultivating Patience and Persistence

_____

_____

_____

_____

_____

_____

My Weekly Prayer

I Pray for Cultivating Patience and Persistence!

Week 16

Embracing Innovation

Stay open to innovation and change. The world of wealth is dynamic, and embracing new technologies and ideas can lead to breakthroughs in your financial journey.

My Notes for Embracing Innovation

_____

_____

_____

_____

_____

_____

My Weekly Prayer

I Pray for Embracing Innovation!

Week 17

Recognizing Opportunities

Train yourself to spot opportunities in various situations. Often, hidden chances for growth and wealth are right in front of you. Stay curious and open-minded to make the most of these moments.

My Notes for Recognizing Opportunities

_____

_____

_____

_____

_____

_____

My Weekly Prayer

I Pray for Recognizing Opportunities!

Week 18

Mastering the Art of Negotiation

Negotiation skills are invaluable in wealth-building. Whether negotiating a salary, a contract, or a deal, mastering this skill can lead to increased earnings and better financial outcomes.

My Notes for Mastering the Art of Negotiation

_____

_____

_____

_____

_____

_____

_____

My Weekly Prayer

I Pray for Mastering the Art of Negotiation!

Week 19

Creating a Vision Board

Visualize your financial goals by creating a vision board. Compile images and words that represent your desires. Placing this board where you can see it daily will remind you of your aspirations and keep you motivated.

My Notes for Creating a Vision Board

_____

_____

_____

_____

_____

_____

My Weekly Prayer

I Pray for Creating a Vision Board!

Week 20

Practicing Mindful Spending

Practice mindfulness when spending money. Pause and reflect on whether a purchase aligns with your values and goals. Mindful spending fosters a healthier relationship with money and prevents impulsive decisions.

My Notes for Practicing Mindful Spending

_____

_____

_____

_____

_____

_____

_____

My Weekly Prayer

I Pray for Practicing Mindful Spending!

Week 21

Learning from Financial Role Models

Study the lives and strategies of successful individuals in the financial world. Their journeys can provide valuable insights and inspiration as you work toward your own empowerment.

My Notes for Learning from Financial Role Models

_____

_____

_____

_____

_____

_____

_____

My Weekly Prayer

I Pray for Learning from Financial Role Models!

Week 22

Leveraging social media for Business

*E*xplore the power of social media for promoting your business or personal brand. It's a cost-effective way to reach a wide audience and connect with potential clients or customers.

My Notes for Leveraging social media for Business.

_____

_____

_____

_____

_____

_____

_____

<ins>*My Weekly Prayer*</ins>

I Pray for Leveraging social media for Business!

Week 23

Investing in Knowledge

Invest in your education and skill development. The more you know, the more you can offer in terms of value, whether in your career or entrepreneurial ventures.

My Notes for Investing in Knowledge

_____

_____

_____

_____

_____

_____

My Weekly Prayer

I Pray for Investing in Knowledge!

Week 24

Letting Go of Financial Regrets

*R*elease any past financial regrets or mistakes. Dwelling on them only holds you back. Instead, focus on the lessons learned and use them to make better decisions moving forward.

My Notes for Letting Go of Financial Regrets

_____

_____

_____

_____

_____

_____

_____

My Weekly Prayer

I Pray for Letting Go of Financial Regrets!

Week 25

Building a Strong Credit Profile

Maintain a strong credit profile by paying bills on time and managing your credit responsibly. A healthy credit score opens doors to favorable financial opportunities.

My Notes for Building a Strong Credit Profile

_____

_____

_____

_____

_____

_____

_____

My Weekly Prayer

I Pray for Building a Strong Credit Profile!

Week 26

Setting Boundaries Around Money

Establish healthy boundaries around money in your relationships. Open communication and clear expectations help prevent conflicts and empower everyone involved.

My Notes for Setting Boundaries Around Money

_____

_____

_____

_____

_____

_____

_____

<u>*My Weekly Prayer*</u>

I Pray for Setting Boundaries Around Money!

Week 27

Creating Passive Income Streams

Explore ways to generate passive income, such as rental properties, investments, or royalties. Passive income can provide financial security and free up time for other pursuits.

My Notes for Creating Passive Income Streams

_____

_____

_____

_____

_____

_____

_____

My Weekly Prayer

I Pray for Creating Passive Income Streams!

Week 28

Reflecting on Financial Growth

Take time to reflect on how far you've come in your financial journey. Celebrate your achievements and use them as motivation to continue pursuing empowerment.

My Notes for Reflecting on Financial Growth

My Weekly Prayer

I Pray for Reflecting on Financial Growth!

Week 29

Giving Back to the Community

Contribute to your community by volunteering your time, skills, or resources. Giving back fosters a sense of purpose and abundance in your life.

My Notes for Giving Back to the Community

_____

_____

_____

_____

_____

_____

_____

My Weekly Prayer

I Pray for Giving Back to the Community!

Week 30

Practicing Visualization Techniques

Enhance your manifestation abilities through visualization. Close your eyes and vividly imagine your financial goals as already achieved. This practice reinforces your belief in their attainment.

My Notes for Practicing Visualization Techniques

_____

_____

_____

_____

_____

_____

_____

My Weekly Prayer

I Pray for Practicing Visualization Techniques!

Week 31

Setting Intentions for the Month Ahead

*B*egin the month by setting clear intentions for your financial goals. Write down what you aim to accomplish and commit to taking consistent actions toward your empowerment.

My Notes for Setting Intentions for the Month Ahead

_____

_____

_____

_____

_____

_____

_____

My Weekly Prayer

I Pray for Setting Intentions for the Month Ahead!

Week 32

Embracing Change for Prosperity

*W*elcome change as a catalyst for growth. *Embracing new opportunities and adapting to shifts in your financial landscape can lead to greater prosperity.*

My Notes for Embracing Change for Prosperity

_____

_____

_____

_____

_____

_____

_____

My Weekly Prayer

I Pray for Embracing Change for Prosperity!

Week 33

Setting Financial Milestones

Break down your larger financial goals into achievable milestones. Celebrate each milestone reached as you move steadily toward your ultimate vision of empowerment.

My Notes for Setting Financial Milestones

_____

_____

_____

_____

_____

_____

_____

My Weekly Prayer

I Pray for Setting Financial Milestones!

Week 34

Building a Supportive Network

Surround yourself with individuals who uplift and support your financial journey. A strong network can provide guidance, collaboration, and a sense of community.

My Notes for Building a Supportive Network

_____

_____

_____

_____

_____

_____

_____

My Weekly Prayer

I Pray for Building a Supportive Network!

Week 35

Exploring New Ventures

*V*enture into new territories that align with your interests and skills. Exploring fresh avenues can lead to unexpected wealth-building opportunities.

My Notes for Exploring New Ventures

_____

_____

_____

_____

_____

_____

_____

My Weekly Prayer

I Pray for Exploring New Ventures!

Week 36

Mastering Time Management

Efficiently manage your time to balance work, personal life, and wealth-building activities. Prioritize tasks that align with your goals to maximize productivity.

My Notes for Mastering Time Management

_____

_____

_____

_____

_____

_____

_____

My Weekly Prayer

I Pray for Mastering Time Management!

Week 37

Navigating Economic Cycles

Understand that economic cycles are natural. Position yourself to benefit from both upswings and downturns by staying informed and making strategic decisions.

My Notes for Navigating Economic Cycles

_____

_____

_____

_____

_____

_____

_____

My Weekly Prayer

I Pray for Navigating Economic Cycles!

Week 38

Rewriting Your Money Story

*I*dentify and transform any limiting beliefs about money. Replace them with affirmations that reinforce your worthiness of financial abundance. Attuned to market trends and consumer preferences. Being informed positions you to seize opportunities and innovate within your industry.

My Notes for Rewriting Your Money Story

_____

_____

_____

_____

_____

_____

My Weekly Prayer

I Pray for Rewriting Your Money Story!

Week 39

Expressing Gratitude for Finances

Practice gratitude specifically for your financial situation. Acknowledging your current wealth opens the path for more abundance to flow in.

My Notes for Expressing Gratitude for Finances

_____

_____

_____

_____

_____

_____

_____

My Weekly Prayer

I Pray for Expressing Gratitude for Finances!

Week 40

Investing in Relationships

Invest time in building and nurturing relationships. Genuine connections can lead to collaborations, partnerships, and new avenues for financial growth.

My Notes for Investing in Relationships

_____

_____

_____

_____

_____

_____

_____

<u>My Weekly Prayer</u>

I Pray for Investing in Relationships!

Week 41

Diversifying Investment Portfolios

Explore a variety of investment options to minimize risk and optimize returns. Diversification is key to creating a stable and growing portfolio.

My Notes for Diversifying Investment Portfolios

_____

_____

_____

_____

_____

_____

_____

My Weekly Prayer

I Pray for Diversifying Investment Portfolios!

Week 42

Embodying Confidence

Cultivate unshakable self-confidence. Believe in your ability to create wealth and navigate any challenges that come your way.

My Notes for Embodying Confidence

_____

_____

_____

_____

_____

_____

_____

My Weekly Prayer

I Pray for Embodying Confidence!

Week 43

Identifying Market Trends

Stay attuned to market trends and consumer preferences. Being informed positions you to seize opportunities and innovate within your industry.

My Notes for Identifying Market Trends

_____

_____

_____

_____

_____

_____

_____

My Weekly Prayer

I Pray for Identifying Market Trends!

Week 44

Crafting a Compelling Brand

Build a strong personal or business brand that communicates value and authenticity. A compelling brand attracts clients, customers, and financial opportunities.

My Notes for Crafting a Compelling Brand

_____

_____

_____

_____

_____

_____

_____

My Weekly Prayer

I Pray for Crafting a Compelling Brand!

Week 45

Calculated Risk Taking

*E*valuate risks carefully and take calculated leaps. Bold actions can lead to breakthroughs and accelerate your entrepreneurial journey.

My Notes for Calculated Risk Taking

_____

_____

_____

_____

_____

_____

_____

My Weekly Prayer

I Pray for Calculated Risk Taking!

Week 46

Fostering Resilience

Evaluate risks carefully and take calculated leaps. Bold actions can lead to breakthroughs and accelerate your entrepreneurial journey.

My Notes for Fostering Resilience

_____

_____

_____

_____

_____

_____

_____

My Weekly Prayer

I Pray for Fostering Resilience!

Week 47

Customer Centric Approach

*P*rioritize delivering value to your customers. A customer-centric approach fosters loyalty, referrals, and sustained business growth.

My Notes for Customer Centric Approach

_____

_____

_____

_____

_____

_____

_____

My Weekly Prayer

I Pray for A Customer Centric Approach!

Week 48

Setting a Legacy Intention

Consider the legacy you want to leave behind. Align your financial decisions with your values and the impact you wish to make on future generations.

My Notes for Setting a Legacy Intention

_____

_____

_____

_____

_____

_____

_____

My Weekly Prayer

I Pray for A Setting a Legacy Intention!

Week 49

Learning from Failures

View failures as opportunities for improvement. Embrace them as valuable lessons that ultimately contribute to your long-term success.

My Notes for Learning from Failures

_____

_____

_____

_____

_____

_____

_____

My Weekly Prayer

I Pray for Learning from Failures!

Week 50

Planning for Retirement

Start planning for retirement early. Consistent contributions to retirement accounts ensure a comfortable and empowered future.

My Notes for Planning for Retirement

_____

_____

_____

_____

_____

_____

_____

My Weekly Prayer

I Pray for Planning for Retirement!

Week 51

Pursuing Lifelong Learning

Embrace learning as a lifelong pursuit. New skills and knowledge can open doors to unexpected opportunities and wealth.

My Notes for Pursuing Lifelong Learning

_____

_____

_____

_____

_____

_____

_____

My Weekly Prayer

I Pray for the Pursuit of Lifelong Learning!

Week 52

Give Thanks unto God!

Give thanks unto God for bringing from week 1 to week 52. Praise Him for your strength, knowledge gained, and discipline obtained during this 1-year period.

My Notes for Giving Thanks unto God

_____

_____

_____

_____

_____

_____

My Weekly Prayer

I Pray for all that God has done to improve my life this year.!

10
Scripture References

1. **Malachi 3:10:** "Bring the whole tithe into the storehouse, that there may be food in my house. Test me in this," says the Lord Almighty, "and see if I will not throw open the floodgates of heaven and pour out so much blessing that there will not be room enough to store it." (NIV)

2. **Proverbs 3:9-10:** "Honor the Lord with your wealth, with the first fruits of all your crops; then your barns will be filled to overflowing, and your vats will brim over with new wine." (NIV)

3. **Matthew 6:33:** "But seek first his kingdom and his righteousness, and all these things will be given to you as well." (NIV)

4. **Proverbs 22:7:** "The rich rule over the poor, and the borrower is slave to the lender." (NIV)

5. **Luke 6:38:** *"Give, and it will be given to you. A good measure, pressed down, shaken together and running over, will be poured into your lap. For with the measure you use, it will be measured to you." (NIV)*

6. **Proverbs 13:11:** *"Dishonest money dwindles away, but whoever gathers money little by little makes it grow." (NIV)*

7. **Ecclesiastes 5:10:** *"Whoever loves money never has enough; whoever loves wealth is never satisfied with their income. This too is meaningless." (NIV)*

8. **Deuteronomy 8:18:** *"But remember the Lord your God, for it is he who gives you the ability to produce wealth." (NIV)*

9. **Psalm 112:5:** *"Good will come to those who are generous and lend freely, who conduct their affairs with justice." (NIV)*

10. **Philippians 4:19:** *"And my God will meet all your needs according to the riches of his glory in Christ Jesus." (NIV)*

Goal Setting

My Goal Is:

_____

_____

Timeframe:

From _____ **to** _____

1. Define Your Goal: *Describe your goal in specific terms. What is the outcome you want to achieve? Be clear and concise.*

2. Why is This Goal Important to You? *Identify the reasons behind your goal. How will achieving this goal positively impact your life?*

3. Break it Down: *Divide your goal into smaller, actionable steps. What are the milestones or checkpoints along the way?*

4. Set a Deadline for Each Step: *Assign deadlines to each of the smaller steps. When will you accomplish each milestone?*

5. Resources Needed: List the resources required to achieve your goal. This could include time, money, skills, tools, or support.

6. Challenges: Anticipate obstacles that may arise. What challenges could hinder your progress, and how will you overcome them?

7. Stay Motivated: Write down ways you'll stay motivated throughout your journey. This could include rewards, reminders, or accountability partners.

8. Measure Your Progress: How will you track your progress? Consider using metrics, tracking tools, or journaling to document your achievements.

9. Celebrate Achievements: Plan how you'll celebrate reaching milestones along the way. Recognizing your progress boosts morale and motivation.

10. Adjust and Adapt: As you move forward, be open to adjusting your plan if necessary. Flexibility allows you to respond to changes and stay on track.

11. Final Reflection: Write a brief reflection on completing this goal. What did you learn from the process, and how will you apply this to future goals?

Remember, your goals should be SMART: Specific, Measurable, Achievable, Relevant, and Time-bound.

NOTES

About The Author

Dr. G. R. Quarles is an experienced and accomplished author, lecturer, and workshop facilitator who has dedicated his career to promoting financial management and wealth building for individuals, businesses, non-profits, and churches. With over 30 years of experience in corporate and government positions, he brings a wealth of knowledge and expertise to his work in the field of financial management.

Dr. Quarles has also served as an adjunct college professor of management, economics, finance, and supply chain for over 20 years at Virginia Union University Sydney Lewis School of Business, Richmond, Virginia and has made a significant contribution to the education of future business leaders. His experience in ministry, including 15 years as the Pastor of Mt. Sinai Baptist Church, King William, Virginia, has given him a unique perspective on the challenges and opportunities faced by African American churches.

As a guest lecturer, workshop facilitator, and certification instructor, Dr. Quarles has helped countless individuals, organizations, and churches to improve their financial management practices and achieve their goals. His commitment to effective stewardship and long-term financial stability has made him a trusted and respected voice in the field of financial management.

Overall, Dr. Quarles' wealth of experience and dedication to financial management and wealth building make him an asset to any organization seeking to improve its financial practices and achieve its goals.

Made in the USA
Middletown, DE
30 October 2023

41574063R00050